The Ar

Co-created by
Kristine Landon-Smith
and
Sita Brahmachari

Based on the illustrated novel by
Shaun Tan

Directed by
Kristine Landon-Smith

Script by
Sita Brahmachari

Methuen Drama

Bloomsbury Methuen Drama

An imprint of Bloomsbury Publishing Plc

50 Bedford Square	175 Fifth Avenue
London	New York
WC1B 3DP	NY 10010
UK	USA

www.bloomsbury.com

Co-created by Kristine Landon-Smith and Sita Brahmachari
Based on the illustrated novel *The Arrival* by Shaun Tan

The Arrival was first published in 2007 by Hodder
This adaptation was first published in 2013 by Methuen Drama

British Library Cataloguing-in-Publication Data
A catalogue record for this book is available from the British Library

ISBN
PB: 978-1-4725-3500-9
ePDF: 978-1-4725-3507-8
ePub: 978-1-4725-3506-1

Typeset by Country Setting, Kingsdown, Kent CT14 8ES
Printed and bound in Great Britain

tamasha

Tamasha and Circus Space present

the ARRIVAL

co-created by
Kristine Landon-Smith *and* **Sita Brahmachari**

based on the illustrated novel by
Shaun Tan

directed by
Kristine Landon-Smith

script by
Sita Brahmachari

in association with
Nuffield Theatre, Southampton

 Esmée Fairbairn FOUNDATION   LOTTERY FUNDED

 HIGHER EDUCATION FUNDING COUNCIL FOR ENGLAND   LOTTERY FUNDED   Supported using public funding by ARTS COUNCIL ENGLAND

Asia House Fair

ASIA HOUSE

Explore our lively pop-up Asian marketplace, bringing all the buzz of Kashgar and the Silk Road to Asia House for one long weekend.

Now in its fourth year, 2013 is our largest fair yet.

Over 35 exhibitors have been selected to represent the best in arts, crafts and design from across the Asian region, selling unique and unusual hand-crafted items.

Craft workshops will run over the weekend, drop in and learn some practical skills.

For more information please visit www.asiahouse.org

Friday	10.00 – 18.00
Saturday	10.00 – 18.00
Sunday	11.00 – 16.00

63 New Cavendish Street
London W1G 7LP

12–14 April

Admission Free

Jewellery

Textiles

Furniture

Art

Books

Ornaments

Clothes

Handicrafts

Homeware

the ARRIVAL

a creative journey

Five years ago we turned the pages of Shaun Tan's extraordinary graphic novel depicting migration. To experience the book together took us the whole day, as we paused over the subtlest sepia details and it feels right that the journey to this production has been equally considered, moving forward in stages, sharing ideas, workshopping with circus artists, actors, choreographers, a composer and migrant groups (through iceandfire) and Woven Gold (the Helen Bamber Foundation music group).

The collaboration with Circus Space has indeed afforded us the rare experience as artists to fully explore the territory and boundaries of this piece. We are the children of migrants and what struck us both as we immersed ourselves in Tan's imagery was our own familiarity with the stories – their ever shifting balance between the domestic detail (packing a suitcase or tasting strange fruit) and the epic flights of the imagination required to uproot a life and reinvent yourself in an alien land, language and culture.

Tan's novel offers the reader an insight into the universal story of the human condition that speaks to the heart. It is an evocation of flight and landings of the kinds made every day by migrants into the United Kingdom. Whether they have landed here as refugees or as economic migrants, the bravery of their journeys is always central to the story and often in contrast to the prevailing negative political discourse.

Like the circus artists who can suspend themselves between worlds, make a ribbon or pole into a cocoon, shelter or viewing post, the migrant must make a new world from what he or she can build with only their own hands, minds and hearts. We

have set 'Dele' our 'man with the hat' (who arrived in this country in the 1950s) in a house in Finsbury Park – a house he has built himself in contemporary London, and to which he welcomes generations of newer migrants.

Towards the end of his life he reflects through 'memory's portal' on his experience of leaving his homeland and arriving in the UK and the many migration stories from around the world that echo through the rooms of his hostel. The sparse poetic text that weaves the piece together draws on research, contemporary commentaries, verbatim texts, song, a newly commissioned musical score and visual imagery inspired by Tan's graphic novel.

In this circus-theatre production we have striven to balance the elements and invite you, as Tan does, to make the journey, to fly and fall . . . and tread the path of eternal suspension experienced by migrants throughout the ages.

Sita Brahmachari and Kristine Landon-Smith
Co-creators

I first met Kristine Landon-Smith in spring 2008 when Circus Space launched the Creative Exchange Programme. Creative Exchange was funded by the Jerwood Charitable Foundation and was designed to encourage established directors to work with circus by giving them time and space to workshop ideas with a small group of circus performers.

Kristine snapped up the opportunity to work in this way and proposed a week spent exploring Shaun Tan's graphic novel *The Arrival*. Working with eight circus artists, she wove their skills into Tan's characters and stories and found new meaning in the images they created. We were all excited by the promise in this early research and development.

However, it wasn't until 2011 that we took the next step when *The Arrival* was staged as a student production featuring our entire second year. Circus Space provided the artists, the venue and all the equipment. To these basic ingredients, Tamasha added the skills of Kristine and writer Sita Brahmachari plus a full professional creative team.

The student production was a crucial step. By the autumn of 2011, Sita had the structure for her script, Adam Wiltshire, the designer, had established a strong design aesthetic, significant progress had been made in the design of the projections and the music, and Kristine had a clear idea of the roles and circus skills she wanted to include. At the same time we had delivered a student production that truly challenged ideas of what circus-based theatre could be.

When *The Arrival* goes on tour it will be the first time that Circus Space has collaborated on a full-scale professional touring production. At a time when all arts and educational establishments are being asked to do more for less, this project presents an interesting model for future collaborations between higher education and the professional arts sector. By pooling our resources and our expertise and allowing the production time to grow and flourish, I think we have taken a huge leap forward in what a circus-based theatre production can be. And of course, in many ways, the journey has been as rewarding as *The Arrival*.

Daisy Drury
Director of Circus Development, Circus Space

Thank You
Tamasha would like to thank: all the staff and teachers at Circus Space, the performers, creative and production teams involved with the previous R&Ds and showcases, Frantic Assembly, Illuminate Design, Graeae, Theatre Royal Stratford East and Watford Palace Theatre, Freedom from Torture, the Jerwood Charitable Foundation for supporting the initial Creative Exchange and everyone else who has contributed to the project.

Circus Space is funded by Arts Council England and the Higher Education Funding Council of England.

Ensemble
Antoinette Akodulu, Gisele Edwards, Charlie Folorunsho as Dele, Sam Hague, Antonio Harris, Jackie Le, Nektarios Papadopoulos, Addis Williams.

Creative Team

Co-created by	Kristine Landon-Smith & Sita Brahmachari
Based on the illustrated novel by	Shaun Tan
Director	Kristine Landon-Smith
Script	Sita Brahmachari
Designer	Adam Wiltshire
Choreography	Freddie Opoku-Addaie
Visual Design	Yeast Culture
Lighting Designer	Andy Purves
Composer	Felix Cross
Sound Designer	Mike Furness
Circus Consultant	Glen Stewart
Costume Supervisor	Alison Cartledge
Music Group	Woven Gold

For Circus Space

Director of Circus Development	Daisy Drury
Operations Director	Jon Dix

Production Team

Production Manager	Dennis Charles
Company Stage Manager	Roshni Savjani
Deputy Stage Manager	Catherine Gibbs
Technical Stage Manager	David Phillips
Rigger	Tom Ratcliffe
Set building and painting	Visual Scene
Truss and sound equipment	Crosslight & Sound Production Services
Photography	Barry Lewis, Sandra Ciampone
Original illustration	janelaurie.com

Tamasha Developing Artists Creative Projects & Collaborations

Write to Life Coordinator	Sheila Hayman
Artistic Director, iceandfire	Christine Bacon
Assistant Director (Write to Life)	Melanie Spencer
Assistant Lighting Designer	Zoe Spurr
Writing Bursary	Michelle Thomas
Digital Bursary	Eva Auster
Extended Observership	Andrea Milde
Observers	Lisa Peck, Kaveh Rahnama, John Walton

tamasha

Tamasha means 'commotion', creating a stir.

Tamasha is an award-winning theatre company which has played a key role in driving the crossover of culturally specific work into the British mainstream. The company was founded in 1989 by Kristine Landon-Smith and actor/playwright Sudha Bhuchar.

Successes like *East is East, Strictly Dandia* and most recently *Snookered* have won acclaim from audiences and critics alike.

The company curiously investigates personal stories and cultural difference and connection as rich and radical sources for theatre, nurturing today's unknown talent to become tomorrow's leading artists by delivering bespoke training and tangible professional opportunities with its Tamasha Developing Artists (TDA) programme.

'I am a writer and without Tamasha I'd still be a taxi-driver. My voice as a northern Asian would be muted and my attempts to open a window on a largely unexplored world would be firmly shut.'

Ishy Din, writer of *Snookered*

'Tamasha means commotion, creating a stir, and the company is certainly doing that.'

What's on Stage on *Snookered*

www.tamasha.org.uk

Artistic Directors	Sudha Bhuchar & Kristine Landon-Smith
General Manager	Julia Good
Marketing Manager	Clare Callan
TDA Project Manager/Producer	Valerie Synmoie
Finance Officer	Jane Porter
Producing Assistant	Felicity Davidson
Press Consultant	Nancy Poole
Fundraising Consultant	Rachel Parslew
TDA Scratch Producer	Alia Alzougbi
Administrative Assistant	Cathy Conneff

Board
Tom Bewick (Chair), Anuj J Chande, Shernaz Engineer, Sumi Ghose, Nishma Gosrani, Zachary Latif, Ramesh K Vala OBE

Support Us

Since 1989, Tamasha has been making an invaluable contribution to British theatre with its vibrant, award-winning productions. We have launched the careers of many well-known artists such as Parminder Nagra (*Bend it Like Beckham*), Jimi Mistry (*West is West*) and Raza Jaffrey (*Spooks*), and we continue to nurture the next generation through the Tamasha Developing Artists (TDA) programme.

Our ladder of opportunity from training to employment propels talented artists into the heart of British theatre. If you would like to form a closer relationship with Tamasha and artists such as Ishy Din, we are launching a TDA bursary and commissioning fund, thus ensuring that we continue to 'create a stir'.

£250 will subsidise a TDA artist on a Tamasha course.

£500 will ensure an individual bursary for developing early ideas like previous shows *auntie netta* and *All I Want is a British Passport!*

£1000 will fund a TDA artist-led initiative leading to a scratch performance.

£5000 plus will invite you into the heart of the company, linking your name to specific artists and projects, giving you an insight into the artistic practice from the seed of an idea to the finished piece.

'I found a power from using my own cultural background in the TDA laboratory. It was liberating, powerful and I gained confidence.'
                                                            Silvana Montoya, actor

To find out more about these opportunities and unique benefits, please contact Sudha on friends@tamasha.org.uk or 0207 749 0090.

Tamasha is funded by Arts Council England and gratefully acknowledges financial support from The Esmée Fairbairn Foundation and its Friends and Patrons. *The Arrival* is kindly supported by the National Lottery through the Big Lottery Fund, The Idlewild Trust and Unity Theatre Trust.

Tamasha Friends and Patrons: Anant Shah (President of the Friends), Aarti Bhanderi, Matt Carter, Milan & Gita Chauhan, Régis Cochefert, Shernaz Engineer, Stella & Daniel Flowers, Mukesh & Kundan Gohil, GV Films Limited, Saad Haafiz, Mobeen Jassat, Azam Javaid & Shayasta Ashiq, Bir & Gerlinde Kathuria, Shaheen Khan, Jay Lakhani, Zachary Latif, Nilesh and Nina Majeethia, Luke Mason, Sarah Moorehead, Salil Patankar & Mrs Patankar, Daksha Patel, Lopa Patel, Sanjiv Patel, Shiv & Reena Popat, Brett & Lisa Sainty, Nitin Shah, Anshu Srivastava, Ramesh & Ella Vala, Alan, Linda & Ana Westall together with those who wish to remain anonymous.

The Arrival Collaborators

Tamasha is thrilled to be working with **iceandfire**, **Write to Life** and **Woven Gold** on a series of creative projects and events around the themes of migration and asylum that will accompany performances.

Souvenirs

By Christine Bacon, directed by Kristine Landon-Smith
A Tamasha collaboration with iceandfire and Write to Life

'What happened to me, the marks on my body, the memories, they are going to be my souvenirs.'

Tracy, Write to Life participant

Some performances of *The Arrival* will be preceded by *Souvenirs* – a moving, short piece based on the testimony of and performed by participants from Write to Life about their experiences of adapting to life in London and the daily challenges they face.

'Writing Souvenirs was, in essence, a process of getting to know five remarkable individuals who endured the violent repression of their governments and who came to the UK in order to save their lives. I am in awe of their courage.'

Christine Bacon,
Artistic Director, iceandfire
www.iceandfire.co.uk

iceandfire explores human rights stories through performance

Write to Life, Freedom from Torture's creative writing group (the longest running writing group for torture survivors in the world), provides participants with a creative outlet for their experiences and a way to explore the torture from their past and the difficulties of living in exile.

'After our first collaboration with Tamasha around The Arrival *on the short film* Finding a Voice *about performance, it was thrilling to have the chance to put those lessons into practice, in a piece of theatre where our writers tell their own stories, crafted into a powerful script.'*

Sheila Hayman
Write to Life Coordinator
www.freedomfromtorture.org/survivor-voices/5112

Woven Gold, the music group at the Helen Bamber Foundation, has collaborated with Tamasha on the composition of original choral pieces for the production, drawn from traditional community lullabies.

'Woven Gold is made up of refugees escaping cruelty from Kurdistan, Pakistan, Burma, Georgia, Iran and many African countries, led by professional UK musicians who give their time. The opportunity to collaborate with actors and circus artists, contributing their own songs, is an exciting new venture for the group.'

Annie Blaber, Woven Gold
www.helenbamber.org/music-group

circus
space

Circus Space is a registered charity and one of Europe's leading providers of circus education. Based in a magnificent Victorian power station adjacent to Hoxton Square, we involve thousands of people in the creation and performance of circus arts every year.

Our diverse range of work includes the UK's only BA Hons degree in Circus Arts, a structured progressive training programme for under 18s and professional development opportunities for aspiring and established performers. Adults and young people can take part in a range of recreational classes and we provide workshops and away days for the business community.

ⓘ www.circusspace.co.uk

Coronet Street   London   N1 6HD   Follow us on
Facebook, Tumblr, Twitter

Creative Team

SHAUN TAN   Creator of the illustrated novel *The Arrival*
Shaun grew up in the northern suburbs of Perth, Western Australia.
He graduated from the University of WA in 1995 with joint honours
in Fine Arts and English Literature, and currently works full time as a
freelance artist and author in Melbourne. Shaun began drawing and
painting images for science fiction and horror stories in small-press
magazines as a teenager, and has since become best known for
illustrated books that deal with social, political and historical
subjects through surreal, dream-like imagery. Books such as *The
Rabbits*, *The Red Tree*, *Tales from Outer Suburbia* and the acclaimed
wordless novel *The Arrival* have been widely translated and enjoyed
by readers of all ages. Shaun has also worked as a theatre designer,
and worked as a concept artist for the films *Horton Hears a Who*
and Pixar's *WALL-E*, and directed the Academy Award-winning short
film *The Lost Thing* with Passion Pictures Australia. In 2011 he
received the prestigious Astrid Lindgren Memorial Award, honouring
his contribution to international children's literature.

KRISTINE LANDON-SMITH   Co-creator and Director
Kristine is joint founder and Artistic Director of Tamasha and has
directed nearly all of the company's shows. Her production of *East is
East* was nominated for an Olivier Award, and her original production
of *Fourteen Songs' Two Weddings and a Funeral* won the Barclays
Theatre Award for Best New Musical. Other directing credits include
plays for the Royal Court, Bristol Old Vic, Nitro and the Royal Danish
Theatre. Kristine has taught at the Rose Bruford College of Speech
and Drama, the National Institute of Dramatic Art (NIDA) in Sydney,
the National School of Drama in India, Central School of Speech
and Drama and L'Ecole Philippe Gaulier in Paris. Her short film
Midnight Feast was screened at the 11th Raindance Film Festival.
Radio credits include: *A Yearning*, *Women of the Dust* (Radio 4 –
both winners of CRE Race in the Media Awards) and *Lysistrata* (BBC
World Service). Kristine jointly won, with Sudha Bhuchar, the 2005
Asian Women of Achievement Award for Arts and Culture and the
2010 First Women Award in the Tourism and Leisure category. More
recently, Kristine has directed *A Fine Balance* (Hampstead Theatre
and UK tour), a musical *Wuthering Heights* (national tour, 2009),
The House of Bilquis Bibi (national tour, 2010) and *The Trouble with
Asian Men* (Parramasala Festival, Sydney 2012 and UK tours). She
will take up a position as Lecturer in Acting at NIDA in Sydney,
Australia in April 2013.

SITA BRAHMACHARI Co-creator and Writer

Sita was born in Derby in 1966. She has a BA in English Literature and an MA in Arts Education. Sita's artistic and academic work has explored cultural diversity and representation within the arts. Her writing, research work, community theatre, education projects and plays have been commissioned by among others: the Royal Shakespeare Company, the Royal Court Theatre, the Arts Council, London International Festival of Theatre. Sita has a longstanding relationship with Tamasha through her work in education and writing. Her first commission for Tamasha was *Lyrical MC* (2008). Sita's first novel *Artichoke Hearts* (Macmillan Children's Books) won the Waterstone's Children's Book Award 2011, and was nominated for the Carnegie Medal. Her second novel *Jasmine Skies* was published in March 2012 and has been shortlisted for the Centurion Award and longlisted for the Carnegie Medal. Sita is currently working on her third novel *Kite Spirit* to be published by Macmillan Children's Books in May 2013.

ADAM WILTSHIRE Designer

Adam graduated from the Royal Welsh College of Music and Drama with a First Class Honours in BA Theatre Design and in 2003 he became a group winner of the Linbury Biennial for Theatre Design. He has designed productions for the Royal Ballet including *Tanglewood*, *Sensorium* and *Children of Adam*. Opera designs include *Romeo et Juliette* and *Bluebeards Castle* (Opera North, *Blond Eckbert* and *Birds. Barks. Bones.* (Opera Group) and *Teseo, Promised End, Duenna* (ETO). He has also designed plays for West Yorkshire Playhouse, Watford Palace, The Tron, Theatre Royal Stratford East, Mercury Theatre, the New Wolsey Theatre, Unicorn and the Salisbury Playhouse. Adam has been working with Tamasha on various presentations of *The Arrival* during the last two years of its development.

FREDDIE OPOKU-ADDAIE Choreographer

Freddie is a choreographer, performer, teacher and Artistic Director of Jagged Antics. Born in East London and raised partly in Ghana, his practice draws on elements of folk and gestural dance forms, including gaming rules (with innate indeterminate outcomes). Opoku-Addaie has twice been a finalist at Place Prize with *Silence Speaks Volumes* (2006) and *Fidelity Project* (2010 /11), which was co-created and performed with Frauke Requardt. Opoku-Addaie was a recipient of the Robin Howard Foundation Commission (2009), creating *Mis-thread*, presented at festivals including A Brief Encounter Dance Umbrella (2010). He and Jorge Crecis co-created

Bf, which was on the selected shortlist for Aerowaves Dance Across Europe (2009/10), as well as other works for UK organizations and international festivals including B-Motion (Italy) and Attakkalari India Biennial. He was an Associate Artist of the Royal Opera House (2009–11) and was commissioned to create *Absent Made Present* (2012), which was adapted for rural touring with Dance in Devon. *Absent Made Present* will tour from late 2013–15 with new works.

YEAST CULTURE   Visual Design

Yeast Culture create original and immersive visuals that are projected in live events and installations. They work across art forms and disciplines blending film, live performance, animation, illustration, projection mapping and sound design. For over a decade, the award-winning company has produced work for classical performances, gallery video installations, contemporary dance and theatre productions as well as producing visuals for live bands for world tours. The company is always searching for innovative ways of connecting the stage and the screen into one integrated audience experience. Recent collaborations and shows include Akram Khan, Nitin Sawhney, Ben Orki, Philharmonia Orchestra, Britten Sinfonia, Brian Eno, Esa-Pekka Solonen, Michael Tilson Thomas, Matthew Herbert, George Fenton, Madness, British Council and Jamie Cullum.

The visuals for *The Arrival* were created by Adam Smith and Nick Corrigan.

ANDY PURVES   Lighting Designer

Andy works primarily in visual and movement-based theatre, circus and on projects in found space. He trained in sound and lighting engineering at the University of Derby with an MA in lighting design and theatre-making from CSSD, where he also tutors in lighting. Lighting design projects include: *Gruesome Playground Injuries* (Justin Audibert/The Gate); *Beautiful Burnout* (Frantic Assembly/ National Theatre of Scotland; *Mess* (Caroline Horton); *The Irish Giant* (Cartoon de Salvo); *Little Dogs* (National Theatre Wales/ Frantic Assembly); *Lovesong* (Frantic Assembly); *Stockholm* (Sydney Theatre Company/Frantic Assembly); *Babel* (Stan Won't Dance); *The Erpingham Camp* (Hydrocracker/Brighton Festival); *Ida Barr and Office Party* (Barbican); *Frankenstein* (Northampton Royal); *Home Inverness* (National Theatre of Scotland); and *Outre and Ren-Sa* (Array). He designs regularly for Circus Space, toured extensively with Propeller, Frantic Assembly, the National Theatre of Scotland and Spymonkey, worked for the Brighton, Greenwich and Docklands Festivals, and on *La Clique* and *La Soirée* at the Roundhouse and in the West End.

FELIX CROSS   Composer

Felix has been Artistic Director of Nitro/Black Theatre Co-operative since 1996 for whom he has written, composed and directed many productions including: *Iced* (director); *Passports to the Promised Land* (book, music, lyrics); *Slamdunk* (book, co-director); *An African Cargo* (Director); *An Evening of Soul Food* (director); *The Wedding Dance* (book, co-director); *Mass Carib* (composer, director); and *Desert Boy* (composer, director).

Other works include: *Blues for Railton* (book, music, lyrics – Albany Empire); *Glory!* (Book, music, lyrics – Temba; winner LWT Plays on Stage award); *Integration Octet* (composer – Aldeburgh); *The Bottle Imp* (music – Major Road); *Jekyll and Hyde* (music, lyrics – Major Road); *Macbeth, Talking to Terrorists, O Go My Man, The Overwhelming, Convicts Opera, Mixed Up North* (all for Out of Joint); *Strictly Dandia, A Fine Balance, Wuthering Heights* (co-composed and lyrics) and *The House of Bilquis Bibi* (all for Tamasha); and *Moon on a Rainbow Shawl* (composer, National Theatre).

Music for other productions includes: *Agathon* (23 Agatha Christie plays, Palace Theatre, Westcliff-on-Sea), as well for Nottingham Playhouse, Chichester Festival Theatre, Tricycle Theatre, Gate Theatre, Southwark Playhouse and Hampstead Theatre. He has also composed regularly for BBC Radio 4 and World Service and has directed plays for Greenwich Theatre and Radio 4 Drama. In summer 2012 he was awarded an MBE for services to musical theatre.

MIKE FURNESS   Sound Designer

Mike's theatre sound designs include: *Uncle Vanya* (Lyric Theatre, Belfast, 2012); *The Arrival* (Tamasha, Royal Festival Hall 2012); *The Trouble With Asian Men* (Tamasha, Edinburgh Festival 2011); *Bea* (Soho Theatre); *The House of Bilquis Bibi* (Tamasha, Hampstead Theatre); *Pressure Drop* (Wellcome Collection); *Wuthering Heights* (Tamasha, Lyric Hammersmith); *Deepcut* (Sherman Cymru/BBC Radio 4); *The Changeling* (ETT/Nottingham Playhouse); *Sweet Cider* (Tamasha, Arcola Theatre); *A Fine Balance* (Tamasha, Hampstead Theatre); *Someone Else's Shoes* (ETT/Soho Theatre); *On Emotion, On Religion* (ON Theatre/Soho Theatre); *All's Well That Ends Well, As You Like It* (RSC); *Mother Courage* (National Theatre); and *Blues in the Night, The Witches, Ladyday, The BFG* and *Entertaining Mr Sloane* (West End).

GLEN STEWART   Circus Consultant

Originally from New Zealand, Glen has an artistic gymnastics background both as a competitor and as a coach/teacher. Since arriving in London in 1999, he has been the Head of Acrobatics for the BA (Hons) Degree programme in Circus Arts at Circus Space in London. He has been on a ten-year journey discovering circus arts and how his acrobatic knowledge can be transferred to the wide variety of circus disciplines as a tool for play and creativity.

Ensemble

ANTOINETTE AKODULU

After turning her back on a career in programming, Antoinette decided to follow a career in dance, followed by a two-year degree and career in circus. She now specialises in both the static and swinging aerial disciplines, as well as in street dance. She enjoys work which fuses physical performance with a potent narrative, and is looking forward to working on *The Arrival*.

GISELE EDWARDS

Gisele trained at the Central School of Speech & Drama, Circus Space, and L'École Internationale de Théâtre Jacques Lecoq, Paris. Accolades include: commissioned by London Symphony Orchestra (St Luke's); *Juno* in Trevor Nunn's *The Tempest* (Theatre Royal, Haymarket); shortlisted for the European Jeunes Talents competition; shortlisted and winner of Festival of Firsts (Linbury Studios, Royal Opera House, 2010 and 2007); awarded Lauréat at the Résidence au Centre International des Récollets, Paris, and winner of the Jerwood Prize for Circus. She is a founder and (ex-)member of Shunt and has worked with Clod Ensemble, Complicite, Shunt, Scarabeus, f/z productions, the Dante and Kosmos Quartets, and in the Millennium Dome Show.

CHARLIE FOLORUNSHO   Dele

Charlie has worked with many differing theatre companies on his journey: from schools projects to big stages. He's had the fortune to have been in performances all around the UK, Europe, USA, Japan and Lebanon, and has been in shows on beaches, in parks, bank vaults and churches. His influences are Brecht, Howard Barker, The Specials, David Glass, Anne Dennis, James Brown, Sylvia Pankhurst, Aretha Franklin and Samuel Beckett. He has a daughter called Georgia.

SAM HAGUE

Sam is a versatile circus performer. His skills include rope walking, clowning, juggling, music and swing dancing. He is a graduate of Circus Space and has performed extensively for the past ten years. Alongside performing in *The Arrival*, Sam is working as a singer in a band that plays music and performs circus.

ANTONIO HARRIS

Antonio has trained in some of the world's leading contemporary dance schools, including Bejart Ballet (Lausanne) and LCDS (London). He recently graduated from Circus Space with great achievements. He specialises in Chinese pole, but also does aerial dance (including dancing horizontally on the columns of Imperial College), aerial cradle and flying trapeze. He hopes to share through his work his various visions on life and the experiences he's lived though.

JACKIE LE

Jackie specialises in corde lisse, silks, cerceau and contortion. She also performs in doubles aerial and walkabout and is a resident performer as a speciality act for the Wam Bam Club (Cafe de Paris). She has performed with: Black Fire Agency, La Reve, 33 Events, Madame Galina's *Vaudeville Nights*, London Digital Circus/The Rubbish Side Show, the Elysian Project, Excess All Areas, *La Wally* (Opera Holland Park), *Cirque des Ames Volées* (ECR Events, Blackpool), Rumpus, Digital Media Awards (Dublin), *Britain's Got Talent*, Circus Space, *Anil Desai's Indian Summer* cabaret, Aircraft Circus Entertainment and White Mischief.

NEKTARIOS PAPADOPOULOS

Nektarios was born and grew up in Athens. In 1999 he taught himself juggling. Two years later he was making a living as a street performer and stilt-walker. After another year he became founding member of street-theatre group Pantum. He trained at Carampa, Madrid, studying juggling, theatre, clowning, acrobatics and tight wire, and graduated with a BA from Circus Space, specialising in Chinese pole. In 2009, whilst trying to explore ways of merging performing acrobatics on the Chinese pole and storytelling, he participated in the research and development of *The Arrival*.

ADDIS WILLIAMS

Addis grew up in South London and has been acting since 2003. He has been involved in art and animation, and alongside creating works, he has always had a passion for physical activities. During his childhood, he played sport, danced and studied parkour, martial arts and fight choreography before training in circus skills.

In Conversation with Shaun Tan

What inspired you to create *The Arrival*? Does your family have a migration story?

Yes, my own family history was definitely a key factor in my being attracted to immigrant tales in the first place. I guess I grew up in a mixed-race family without thinking much of it. Having an Australian mum and Chinese dad was just normal. Sometimes I wonder if that has given me a certain perspective that's been useful later on as an artist and writer, a sense that there's no absolute 'normal', that reality is adjustable. Anyway, Dad has many interesting anecdotes about migrating from Malaysia to Western Australia in the 1960s, which I only appreciated myself once I started travelling internationally as an adult. I also realised that a lot of the things I'm trying to do as an artist, looking at my native environment from a certain objective distance, is something that immigrants are routinely doing anyway. In other words, a way of seeing between artists, writers and immigrants is very similar: an acute awareness of everyday strangeness, a necessary attentiveness to primary experience.

You work in a medium which transcends language. Do words or written stories ever inspire your work?

Yes, very much so. In spite of its 'silence', *The Arrival* began life as a long set of written notes based on researched immigrant stories. I was looking for further anecdotes and trying to find points of intersection – those feelings and situations that seemed universal to all immigrants, like homesickness or bureaucratic troubles, confronting food and difficulty with language or customs. I then tried to extrapolate those universal points of internal and external drama into pictures that might equally relate back to every specific anecdote; and removing words, context and even realism was one way of doing that. I'm actually a very wordy person and originally wanted to be a writer rather than an illustrator as a teenager. It just so happens that I'm often now attracted to stories that are best told visually, and I find these come more naturally to me as well.

Your illustrated novels are enjoyed all over the world. Why do you think they resonate so universally?

I've noticed the older I get, the more interested I am in a minimal approach to telling stories, whether that means stripping back the details or just making them very short. That in turn appears to engender broader appeal. What I think is happening is that I'm intuitively making more allowances for the reader to invest their own imagination into the work, rather than trying to tell them what to imagine (as a younger artist, I mistakenly believed that this was the purpose of art-making, having a 'message'). I think storytelling is not about communication or even resolution of an idea; it's rather about simply inspiring others to consider universal things and feelings in their own way.

How does it feel having your work adapted and interpreted in different mediums as with this piece?

It makes me feel that the work is successful, that it has its own changing life, it grows. You know a story is a good one when it has a certain autonomy to it, as if you are just borrowing ideas to carry for a while, before passing them on to someone else. You don't own or control the material, but instead hope it will evolve, even in unpredictable ways. It's particularly rewarding when that interpretation happens across media, reinventing its form, attracting new ideas, and hopefully reaching a new audience too. There's also a slight concern if you are doing graphic novels that you are working in a certain ghetto of interest, and it's nice to see those boundaries dissolve.

What's next for you? Any forthcoming projects you can tell us about?

I'm working with the producer of our Oscar-winning short film *The Lost Thing* on a feature-length project based on *The Arrival*, although it's still in a very early and speculative phase. This would be yet another interpretation of story concepts that is likely to depart significantly from the original book, simply because the medium is so different – so quite a challenge. Currently I'm finishing work on a new picture book (which does have words, but not many) called *Rules of Summer*. I wasn't so sure what it was about when I started it a couple of years ago, but it seems to deal largely with the paradoxes of many sibling relationships, the odd mix of love and rejection that kids might know particularly well (adults too of course). My wife and I are expecting our first baby in the middle of the year, so that's really the next *big* project!

For more about Shaun Tan and his work, visit
www.shauntan.net

The Arrival

Characters

Dele
Chidi
Tian Mey

All other characters played by members of the ensemble.

Some verbatim texts used with kind permission from Christine Bacon at iceandfire.

The cultural backgrounds of the characters (e.g. Nigerian Woman) are specific to the company performing in the 2013 tour. However, all parts could be played by performers of different backgrounds with slight alterations to context and vocabulary.

Note

◀) indicates passages spoken through pre-recorded audio.

Scene One

House in Finsbury Park, London. Music.

Soundscape of multilingual voices telling stories of arrival.

Projection: Shaun Tan's migrant faces.

Present day. Night time. Downstage there is a room with a bedside table and a chair. On the table is a single photo and a paper bird. **Dele** *walks through the house. He passes* **Vietnamese Woman** *on the stairs; she is shouting on her mobile.*

Dele   Problem?

Vietnamese Woman   My boss, he pay me less. I work six days in factory, every week he pay less. I am going to twist his balls!

Dele *smiles and walks into his room.* **Tian Mey**, *his carer, leads him to sit in the chair. She feeds him and gives him water. She picks up the photograph from the table.*

Tian Mey   Here, Dele, is your wife and son.

◀)) **Tian Mey**   My daughter Xiao Feng she is grown up now. I saw her last time when she was two year old. Now, when we speak she is like stranger to me. Too much distance. She is coming to visit after so much time and I am afraid that I have lost her love. You, Dele, are my first welcome face in this country. You will go to heaven for sure.

She lifts up the paper bird.

You made me this bird. Remember?

It's OK with you, if I prepare room for Xiao? I have been working as housekeeper since eight years old. This my first job I actually enjoy. Fifty-two years old already. So much time is lost.

She begins rocking and singing a lullaby in Mandarin. The song reminds **Dele** *of one from his homeland. He attempts to sing his lullaby in a dry crackly voice.*

Dele (*singing*)
  Olu kulu Ku, Olu Kulu Ku O. O-u-ni a ko ko wa fun.
  Igba wi wa ri, atigba si su, igba wi wa ri atigba si so noo.

Projection: birds flying.

◀)) **Dele**
  Peering through memory's portal
  the giant wings
  of the bird
  call me home
  pulling me away.

  This house I built myself
  this brick and mortar
  these rooms
  a monument to friendship
  founded on faith.

  So many faces
  all flowing here and there
  mix up in my mind
  these stories of
  leaving and arriving with nothing but
  this giant egg of hope.

  Notes of Nigeria
  big family,
  major family,
  resting in the armpit of Africa.

Scene Two

1950s. A football match. Friends gather for the last time to say goodbye to **Dele**. **Chidi**, *his son, enters and the game begins.* **Dele** *enters. The boy, realising that his father is going, leaves the game and climbs a tree. The others continue to play with vigour and* **Dele** *attempts to join the camaraderie but is preoccupied with the impending goodbye to his son. The game finishes. The men say goodbye to their friend.*

Dele *stands beneath the tree.*

Dele
   I will send for you.
   Soon, soon. I will send for you
   Come down and say goodbye.

Chidi *refuses to say goodbye. He stays up the tree, turning away from his father.* **Dele** *takes a paper bird that he had placed under his hat and puts it at the bottom of the tree hoping it will entice* **Chidi** *down. It doesn't.* **Dele** *leaves. Once he is out of sight and earshot,* **Chidi** *climbs higher and higher calling to his father in anguish.*

Chidi   Papa, Papa, Papa.

He twists, turns and skims down the tree. He picks up the bird and climbs back up again. His uncle arrives on a bike and attempts to coax him down by playing a few tricks to distract him. Eventually **Chidi** *is coaxed down from the tree, gets on the bike and his uncle rides him back to his mother's door.*

Scene Three

Ship's horn. Passengers enter with suitcases. The ship's horn sounds again. The passengers look back at the land they may never see again.

Projection: migrating birds.

◀ᴵ⁾ Like the migratory flights of the swallows that circle the world in vast sweeps, covering thousands of miles every spring and autumn, refugees and migrants will make extraordinary journeys in search of work and safety, journeys that on the map seem unnecessary and absurd. But unlike the swallows, which follow the same routes year upon year, the journeys made by refugees can last several years, as they wander apparently without reason, from continent to continent.*

---

* From *Human Cargo: A Journey among Refugees* by Caroline Moorehead (Chatto & Windus, 2005).

The ship's horn sounds again. Passengers move towards the ship. They start to find a place for themselves in preparation for the long journey.

Projection: a dragon's tail and clouds.

Polish Man *is talking incessantly to himself, disturbing the other passengers. He is talking to his Polish friend.* **Greek Man** *and his brother look at him.*

Polish Man   Have you never seen Polish before? We are all in the same boat now!

Ship's horn.

Greek Man *climbs the mast to look out to land for the last time.*

Polish Man   You say goodbye to your wife, don't think she will wait for you!

Vietnamese Woman *cries.* **Dele** *pulls out a photograph which he shows to the woman.*

Dele   My son, my wife, my son.

He shows his ten fingers.

Vietnamese Woman (*in her own language*)   He is ten years old?

Dele   Ten.

Vietnamese Woman   Ten.

Dele   Chidi . . . Chidi. Akindele from Nigeria, Africa.

Vietnamese Woman   Akin . . .

Dele *nods conceding that his name must be shortened.*

Dele.

He pats his chest again.

Dele.

Vietnamese Woman   Thanh Chau.

Dele   Thanh Chau.

Vietnamese Woman *starts to cry and in Vietnamese starts to tell*
Dele *how she has had to leave her child behind. He looks uncomfortable.*
Another female passenger gestures to **Vietnamese Woman** *to return*
to her berth.

◀») **Dele**
  Peering through the ship's portal
  the giant wings of the bird calling me home
  calling me
  pulling me away
  waves roll higher and higher
  falling deeper.

  No mountains.
  No sign of land.
  Only endless sea.
  Endless sea.
  Land is gone.

Darkness falls and the whole ship is lulled to sleep.

A storm. The passengers are thrown about the ship. As the storm builds
the passengers fight for their survival.

Eventually the sea calms. Passengers recover themselves.

◀») **Polish Man** (*starts in Polish, then English*)   I stare and stare
at the sea. Like a great beast ready to eat me whole, swallow
me up. I am trusting this boat to carry me safely on these huge
waves, like a bad-tempered god, becoming angry with us, and
making us suffer. When we get inside the canal the sea is so
rough, I empty everything out of my belly and when there
is nothing left I think the waves will turn me inside out and
that will be the end.

◀») **Dele**   Some days I wonder how many there are just like
me. Thousands, I think, just floating on the oceans right now.
In between our worlds and yours . . . Breathing quietly in the
darkness, hungry, hearing the strange clanking sounds of ships,
smelling the diesel oil and the paint, listening to the bom-bom-
bom of the engines. Wide awake at night, hearing the singing

of whales rising up from the deep sea and vibrating through the ship.

Woman *holding a baby sits up and nurses it.* **Vietnamese Woman** *passenger sits up and looks at her longingly.*

◄» **Vietnamese Woman**   Your future is different to mine. You hold your child close, mine is far away.

The ship's horn sounds. The passengers gather their belongings together and look out at their futures. Those who have made connections with one another hug and say goodbye.

◄» **Dele**   Mists of memory, fog, what did they call it? Smog, fog . . . so dense I felt as if I was falling through clouds. Then through the rain mist I saw it for the first time, just like in a story book, textbook, all glittering, the river flowing through the centre, and I think yes, this is my dream to make a home in this country . . . to bring my wife and son here.

Projection: Shaun Tan imagery of the arrival at the docks.

Scene Four

Dele *and other passengers walk off the ship. They are herded into a queue.* **Dele** *stands in line among the others.*

◄» **Dele**
Wife . . . son
so far away.
No friend.
Only this case I carry with me.
Only these memories of home.
And after so much hope
my heart
falls
falls
falls.
So far down.

🔊 **Greek Man**   People from all over the world and everyone with the same look on their face like they are losing their heart.

🔊 **Vietnamese Woman**   They take your photo, they take your fingerprint, they take your ID, they take your visa, they take your papers and they look at you with this cold grey face you can't see into.

🔊 **Dele**
No home.
No life.
Alien man.
Stranger even to myself.
Stranger.
Hope falls.
So low.
So low.

🔊 **Greek Man**   It could be blank refusal, finished.

🔊 **Nigerian Woman**   My friend told me find good chillies, only then can you survive in this country.

🔊 **Greek Man**   My uncle didn't even know how to cross the zebra crossing when he came here, but now he is black-cab driver. He has mastered the map of London.

🔊 **Polish Man**   I watch this programme *Who Wants To Be a Millionaire?* I know more questions than the English people. I watch and think I will go for it and make my fortune.

Dele *passes through the checkpoint and into this new country.*

Scene Five

A London street. Everything is unfamiliar. **Dele** *looks terrified.*

After some time a man rides by on a bicycle. He notices that **Dele** *appears lost and offers to help him. He picks up* **Dele**'s *case and puts it on the front of his bike.* **Dele** *gets on behind. They ride off.*

◀)) **Dele**
    Just one act of kindness.
    One face to turn to you and smile.
    To say 'yes'.
    I have a place for you to lay your head.

    Step through my door
    my alien friend.
    One pillow.
    Soft feathers under your head.

Scene Six

Present day. House in Finsbury Park. **Tian Mey** *is busy in the house.*

◀)) **Tian Mey**   My daughter is coming . . . I only knew her
baby face . . . I don't even know how tall she is. Which room is
best for her? I don't know. Maybe the sky-blue room at top,
with blue paint, or maybe she likes to be near the garden.

Dele *enters his room and sits. Lodgers enter their bedrooms.*

Dele
    Step through my door
    my friends.
    Step through.

◀)) **Dele**   So many stories in my head, passing through,
passing through.

Sometimes here, sometimes lost.

Tian Mey *enters and repeats exactly the same caring routine that we
saw in the beginning.* **Dele** *is weaker.*

Dele *gestures for her to show him the photo of his wife and son. He
looks at it.*

Dele   Even after all this time, I can't believe they're gone.

On upper level **Al**, *a migrant in the house, walks from his room into
another where a woman is reading. She greets him.*

There is suddenly shouting in the adjacent room. **Al** *puts his hands over his ears as if he expects trouble.*

A spotlight fades up on a room where **Nigerian Woman** *is searching furiously for something. She is swearing in her own language. She leaves her room and knocks furiously on the door of another where* **Al** *and his friend are sitting together.*

Nigerian Woman   I am working here for eight-hour shift, three pounds or four pounds an hour, sometime they don't even pay me. I am still waiting for money they owe me. What do I know about in this country? Lettuce and chicken that is all! Now he steal my visa.

Tian Mey, *who has heard this, comes upstairs, guides the woman back to her room and settles her on her bed. She sits beside her.*

Tian Mey   I told her many times, 'Madam, I don't want to work here, I need to go to Beijing to find my daughter', but they had my passport. They locked it away in a cupboard, like they locked me away. If the doctor did not see me I don't know maybe I will still be in the prison there. He tell her, 'Why you starving this woman?' This made she more angry. She say 'I not give you a ticket, I not give you salary. Just go.' And she threw me on to the street.

When **Tian Mey** *looks down at* **Nigerian Woman**, *she sees that she is fast asleep. The house has grown still. She turns out the light. It is night time. The house is in darkness.* **Tian Mey** *walks over to the window and holds out her hand . . . Snow has begun to fall.*

Projection: snow.

◀)) **Tian Mey**   First time I saw it I was afraid to step into it wearing only my sandals. My toes were frozen. I thought this is a cold cold country.

Passage of time.

Scene Seven

Alarm clock sounds.

Dele

Chidi, Chidi,
my son.
Chidi, Chidi,
my son.
Come down and say goodbye.
I will send for you.
Come now and say goodbye

He is in the throes of a violent nightmare. **Tian Mey** *comes and quietens him.*

Tian Mey   Everywhere you see your wife, your son. Never even said goodbye.

Dele

No sounds in the street.
The house is so quiet.
Where has everyone gone?
Hard work.
Night and day.
No matter.
Work.
Work.
Building, building, building.
Just like me.
This house
I have built myself
with these hands.
This house
these bricks and mortar

He lifts his hands up and inspects them as if they belong to someone else.

Scene Eight

Cockle picking. The following audio text is interspersed with occasional live callings between the workers.

◀)) **Nigerian Woman**   Dig in sand, scoop the cockles, turn them over, brush them down.

Dig in sand, scoop the cockles, turn them over, brush them down.

◀)) **Vietnamese Woman**   Get rid of the feathers, dip chicken in the wax . . . Get rid of the hair, pick the lettuce, strip the leaf, scoop the cockles, turn them over, protect the heart.

◀)) **Al**   Someone got me on a boat. Never knew their names. Africans, Somalians, other Sudanese, you just sit, just you and the big sea. Sardines, water and some bread. Days and days pass on the sea.

◀)) **Vietnamese Woman**   Pick the lettuce, strip the leaf, turn them over, protect the heart. Get rid of the feathers, dip chicken in the wax . . . get rid of the hair, scoop the cockles, turn them over.

◀)) **Nigerian Man**   Dig in sand, scoop the cockles, turn them over, brush them down.

Dig in sand, scoop the cockles, turn them over, brush them down.

◀)) **Al**
    Twelve years old.
    Yes
    twelve.
    This is not a fairy story.
    Two years I am in their prison.
    When I walk out into light my eyes are dazzled
    and my ears are deafened.

I even grow a moustache! Everywhere I look I see my mother, my brother, but when I call to them they turn and it's always some other face.

🔊 **Vietnamese Woman**   One and half years I live in lettuce field. Six people, one caravan. Lettuce . . . make you feel tired. Then on bus . . . the perfume is so strong . . . the perfume they wear gives me headaches.

🔊 **Nigerian Woman**   Dig in sand, scoop the cockles, turn them over, brush them down.

Dig in sand, scoop the cockles, turn them over, brush them down.

Audio develops to a sound collage of all the above.

Scene Nine

Dele *is sitting waiting. He is fully dressed.* **Tian Mey** *comes and starts to lay a table. The inhabitants of the house, dressed for a party, come in with a cake singing 'Happy Birthday'. With great effort,* **Dele** *manages to blow out the candles. They all clap. Now* **Tian Mey** *sings a song of thanks to him for everything he has done for them – the same song she sang at the beginning. Then to everyone's amazement* **Dele** *finds the energy to sing his Nigerian lullaby. They applaud him. One of the inhabitants puts on some party music. They celebrate.*

Projection: Shaun Tan imagery of a man looking over the city.

🔊 **Dele**
I have become the ancient owl of this city.
I sit in watch.
I listen.

The doorbell rings, breaking the atmosphere.

Tian Mey *stands up, shocked, emotional and apprehensive about meeting her daughter for the first time since she was two years old. She walks tentatively towards the door, opens it and a young woman stands before her.*

Silence.

Xiao Feng   Ma Ma.

Tian Mey *traces her hands over her daughter's face, as if she is trying to find in it something of the tiny girl she left behind. After a moment of distance they hug. She takes her hand and invites her into the party. She takes off her rucksack and sits down.* **Tian Mey** *sits next to her, wiping away her tears and holding her daughter's hand. She stares at the woman who sits before her, her daughter who she has not seen since she was a child.*

And so the story of the next arrival begins.

Projection: Shaun Tan's migrant faces.

Methuen Drama Modern Plays

include work by

Edward Albee
Jean Anouilh
John Arden
Margaretta D'Arcy
Peter Barnes
Sebastian Barry
Brendan Behan
Dermot Bolger
Edward Bond
Bertolt Brecht
Howard Brenton
Anthony Burgess
Simon Burke
Jim Cartwright
Caryl Churchill
Complicite
Noël Coward
Lucinda Coxon
Sarah Daniels
Nick Darke
Nick Dear
Shelagh Delaney
David Edgar
David Eldridge
Dario Fo
Michael Frayn
John Godber
Paul Godfrey
David Greig
John Guare
Peter Handke
David Harrower
Jonathan Harvey
Iain Heggie
Declan Hughes
Terry Johnson
Sarah Kane
Charlotte Keatley
Barrie Keeffe

Howard Korder
Robert Lepage
Doug Lucie
Martin McDonagh
John McGrath
Terrence McNally
David Mamet
Patrick Marber
Arthur Miller
Mtwa, Ngema & Simon
Tom Murphy
Phyllis Nagy
Peter Nichols
Sean O'Brien
Joseph O'Connor
Joe Orton
Louise Page
Joe Penhall
Luigi Pirandello
Stephen Poliakoff
Franca Rame
Mark Ravenhill
Philip Ridley
Reginald Rose
Willy Russell
Jean-Paul Sartre
Sam Shepard
Wole Soyinka
Simon Stephens
Shelagh Stephenson
Peter Straughan
C. P. Taylor
Theatre Workshop
Sue Townsend
Judy Upton
Timberlake Wertenbaker
Roy Williams
Snoo Wilson
Victoria Wood

Methuen Drama Contemporary Dramatists

include

John Arden (two volumes)
Arden & D'Arcy
Peter Barnes (three volumes)
Sebastian Barry
Dermot Bolger
Edward Bond (eight volumes)
Howard Brenton
    (two volumes)
Richard Cameron
Jim Cartwright
Caryl Churchill (two volumes)
Sarah Daniels (two volumes)
Nick Darke
David Edgar (three volumes)
David Eldridge
Ben Elton
Dario Fo (two volumes)
Michael Frayn (three volumes)
David Greig
John Godber (four volumes)
Paul Godfrey
John Guare
Lee Hall (two volumes)
Peter Handke
Jonathan Harvey
    (two volumes)
Declan Hughes
Terry Johnson (three volumes)
Sarah Kane
Barrie Keeffe
Bernard-Marie Koltès
    (two volumes)
Franz Xaver Kroetz
David Lan
Bryony Lavery
Deborah Levy
Doug Lucie

David Mamet (four volumes)
Martin McDonagh
Duncan McLean
Anthony Minghella
    (two volumes)
Tom Murphy (six volumes)
Phyllis Nagy
Anthony Neilsen (two volumes)
Philip Osment
Gary Owen
Louise Page
Stewart Parker (two volumes)
Joe Penhall (two volumes)
Stephen Poliakoff
    (three volumes)
David Rabe (two volumes)
Mark Ravenhill (two volumes)
Christina Reid
Philip Ridley
Willy Russell
Eric-Emmanuel Schmitt
Ntozake Shange
Sam Shepard (two volumes)
Wole Soyinka (two volumes)
Simon Stephens (two volumes)
Shelagh Stephenson
David Storey (three volumes)
Sue Townsend
Judy Upton
Michel Vinaver
    (two volumes)
Arnold Wesker (two volumes)
Michael Wilcox
Roy Williams (three volumes)
Snoo Wilson (two volumes)
David Wood (two volumes)
Victoria Wood

Methuen Drama Modern Classics

Jean Anouilh *Antigone* • Brendan Behan *The Hostage* • Robert Bolt
A Man for All Seasons • Edward Bond *Saved* • Bertolt Brecht *The
Caucasian Chalk Circle* • *Fear and Misery in the Third Reich* • *The Good
Person of Szechwan* • *Life of Galileo* • *The Messingkauf Dialogues* •
Mother Courage and Her Children • *Mr Puntila and His Man Matti* •
The Resistible Rise of Arturo Ui • *Rise and Fall of the City of
Mahagonny* • *The Threepenny Opera* • Jim Cartwright *Road* • *Two &
Bed* • Caryl Churchill *Serious Money* • *Top Girls* • Noël Coward
Blithe Spirit • *Hay Fever* • *Present Laughter* • *Private Lives* • *The Vortex* •
Shelagh Delaney *A Taste of Honey* • Dario Fo *Accidental Death of an
Anarchist* • Michael Frayn *Copenhagen* • Lorraine Hansberry *A
Raisin in the Sun* • Jonathan Harvey *Beautiful Thing* • David Mamet
Glengarry Glen Ross • *Oleanna* • *Speed-the-Plow* • Patrick Marber
Closer • *Dealer's Choice* • Arthur Miller *Broken Glass* • Percy Mtwa,
Mbongeni Ngema, Barney Simon *Woza Albert!* • Joe Orton
Entertaining Mr Sloane • *Loot* • *What the Butler Saw* • Mark Ravenhill
*Shopping and F***ing* • Willy Russell *Blood Brothers* • *Educating Rita* •
Stags and Hens • *Our Day Out* • Jean-Paul Sartre *Crime Passionnel* •
Wole Soyinka • *Death and the King's Horseman* • Theatre Workshop
Oh, What a Lovely War • Frank Wedekind • *Spring Awakening* •
Timberlake Wertenbaker *Our Country's Good*